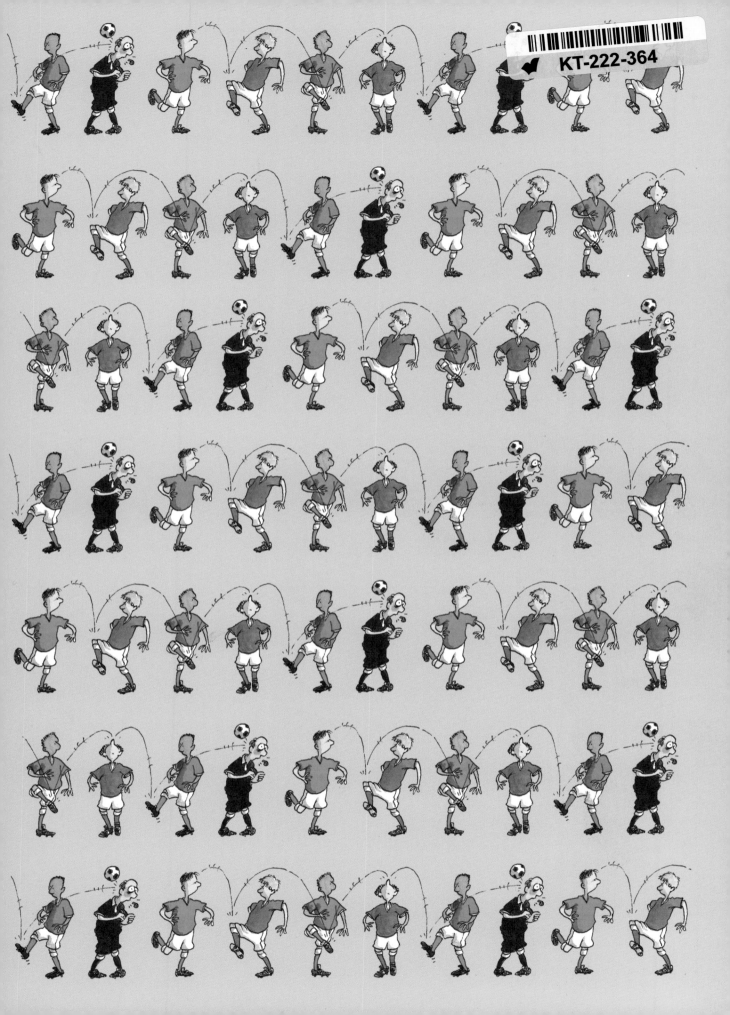

GREAT BIG QUIZ BOOK

MICHAEL COLEMAN

www.michael-coleman.com

Illustrated by
Mike Phillips

SCHOLASTIC

Scholastic Children's Books,
Commonwealth House, 1-19 New Oxford Street
London WC1A 1NU, UK

A division of Scholastic Ltd
London ~ New York ~ Toronto ~ Sydney ~ Auckland
Mexico City ~ New Delhi ~ Hong Kong

First published in the UK by Scholastic Ltd, 2001

Text copyright © Michael Coleman, 2001
Illustrations copyright © Mike Phillips, 2001

ISBN 0 439 99223 0

All rights reserved
Typeset by TW Typesetting, Midsomer Norton, Somerset
Printed by WS Bookwell

2 4 6 8 10 9 7 5 3 1

Contents

INTRODUCTION

Football is full of facts. Some are foul, some are fantastic – and, let's face it, some are fiendishly difficult. The trouble is, it always seems to be the fiendishly difficult ones that other fanatical fans (like your mates) ask you questions about...

Because professional football has been played for well over a hundred years, they'll boringly bombard you with deadly dates as well:

If you know a fan like that then ... congratulations! Because the book you're now holding is going to give you a chance to hit back with questions they won't be able to answer – questions about the foul and fascinating facts that make football such a glorious game!

Scary questions like:

or low-down questions like:

So if you want to discover the funniest football facts, read on! They're foul!

FOUL FOOTBALL HISTORY

1 Here's an easy question to start you off with. What did the nineteenth-century playwright Oscar Wilde say about football? Just fill in the gaps in this quotation:

FOOTBALL IS ALL VERY WELL AS A GAME FOR ROUGH (a) . . . . BUT IT'S HARDLY SUITABLE FOR DELICATE (b) . . . .

(Clue: the two missing words are *boys* and *girls*)

Answer:

1 a – girls; b – boys. (He was being funny.)

Rough rules

Fouls in football are what you call breaking the rules. But what are the rules of football? They've changed a bit since Oscar Wilde's time.

See if you can sort out the fair from the foul in this collection...

2 It's 1878. A player takes a throw-in with one hand. Fair or foul?
3 It's 1888. A goalkeeper is about to save a shot when suddenly he's charged over by one of the other team with the result that the ball sails into the goal. **Fair or foul?**
4 It's 1892. The ball is passed back to the goalkeeper and he picks it up. **Fair or foul?**
5 It's 1902. A player runs out on to the pitch and you can see his knees. **Fair or foul?**
6 It's 1907. A goalkeeper dives off his line before a penalty is taken. **Fair or foul?**

7 It's 1908. The goalkeeper again. This one catches the ball way outside his penalty area, bounces it a few hundred times as he charges up to near the halfway line, then takes a shot at the opposition's goal. **Fair or foul?**

8 It's 1920. A player scores direct from a corner. **Fair or foul?**

Answers:

2 Fair. The two-hands rule was introduced in the 1880s, because some players were able to hurl the ball miles with one hand.

3 Fair. Charging a goalkeeper, even when he didn't have the ball, was allowed until 1890.

4 Fair. This didn't become a foul for another 100 years!

5 Foul. Until 1904 there was a Football Association rule saying that shorts had to reach below a player's knees.

6 Foul. It was allowed until 1905 ... and it's been allowed since 1997! In between, it wasn't.

7 Fair. Until 1912 a goalkeeper could catch the ball anywhere in his own half. One of the players who caused the rule to be changed was Portsmouth's Matthew Reilly. He'd played Gaelic football in Ireland (in which players can run with the ball while they're bouncing it) and once he caught the ball, nobody could get it off him!

8 Foul. This wasn't allowed until 1924.

Football firsts

Every football feature was first featured sometime. Can you work out which of these pairs of football features was featured in football first?

9

Answers:

9–b) The referee's whistle was first heard in 1878, on Notts Forest's ground. Shirt numbers didn't arrive in the football league until 60 years later, in 1939, when both Arsenal and Chelsea wore them in league games.

10–a) Although goalkeepers were known as "net-minders" for a while, the term goalkeeper was used from around 1870 – it had to be, goal nets weren't invented until 1891! Special goalkeepers' jerseys arrived in 1908; until then goalkeepers had worn the same shirts as the rest of their team – very confusing!

11–a) A Nottingham Forest player, Sam Widdowson, invented shinguards in 1874. But heads were thought more valuable than shins – for the first five seasons of the Football League, until 1893, heading the ball was banned.

12–b) The word "soccer" was first used in 1889. White footballs didn't appear in league matches until 1951!

FOUL FOOTBALL CLUBS

'Orrible origins

Football is an eleven-a-side team game – which means that if you want to play the game properly the first thing you've got to find is another ten players to join you.

That's exactly how most of today's big-name football clubs got started. They were formed by groups of old school friends or work-mates or whoever, deciding that they wanted to play this new-fangled game called football.

Match these names of clubs with their fascinating start-up facts: Celtic, Coventry City, FK Austria, Fulham, Juventus, Notts County, Leyton Orient, Sheffield Wednesday, Sunderland, West Ham.

13 They were formed by a group of teachers.
14 They were formed by shop-assistants who had to work all day every Saturday and could only play on their early closing day during the week.
15 They were formed by workers at a bicycle factory.
16 They started life as a church team.
17 They were formed in 1904 by a group of workers at the yard which built HMS Warrior, the first warship made with iron.

18 They were formed as a cricket and football club in the 1890s by some Englishmen who'd gone to live in another country. The cricket didn't catch on, but the football did!

19 They were formed in 1897 by a group of students.

20 They were formed in 1888 by two local businessmen and a Catholic priest named Brother Wilfred. For the next 110 years Catholic priests were allowed in to watch their games free of charge!

21 They were formed in 1881 by desk-bound clerks of a shipping company.

22 They were formed in 1862, making them the world's oldest existing football league club. Their early games were against themselves – they had to be, there weren't any other teams to play!

Answers:

13 Sunderland – which is a shortened version of their first name: The Sunderland and District Teachers Association FC!

14 Sheffield Wednesday – although their first name was simply The Wednesday because that was the day of the week they played on.

15 Coventry City – although their first name was Singers FC, after the name of the bicycle company they worked for.

16 Fulham – which is a shortened version of their first name, Fulham St Andrews Sunday School FC.

17 West Ham United – whose first name was Thames Ironworks FC.

18 FK Austria.

19 Juventus – who used to play in red until one of their players came over to England, saw Notts County in their black-and-white stripes, and liked them so much he went back to Italy and talked his team into changing their colours!

20 Celtic.

21 Leyton Orient – although their first name was simply Orient FC, after the shipping company the clerks worked for.

22 Notts County – who are also the most relegated side in the British Football League!

LET'S SWAP STRIPS AND PLAY IN THIS ONE I FOUND IN ENGLAND

WOW! YES!

OR WE COULD WEAR THIS FLORAL DESIGN I MADE MYSELF

Cool colours

What colours should your team wear? That's a problem all clubs have faced. Sometimes they've done it the easy way and copied another club's colours. For example:

● In the 1960s Leeds United changed from a strip of yellow and blue to all white because they were the colours of Real Madrid, the then European Champions, and their manager Don Revie thought it might inspire them to play the same way!

● They were only doing what Tottenham Hotspur did years before. They switched to white shirts and blue shorts in 1899, the year they decided they wanted to look like the top team of that era, Preston North End.

Try these questions on team strips – but don't get shirty if you don't know the answers!

23 Arsenal's shirts are now red and white, but until 1933 only one of those colours featured in their strip. Which one?

24 What don't top Spanish club Barcelona have on their shirts that every other top European side do have?

25 British teams Barnet, Blackpool, Hull, Motherwell, Dundee United and Wolves all play in orange shirts – but what else do they have in common?

26 In 1883, before they switched to plain white, Bolton Wanderers wore white shirts with – what?

27 Everton's first shirts were black with a white stripe; but where did the stripe start, and where did it end?

Answers:

23 Red – the same colour as Nottingham Forest. Why? Because Arsenal's first ever set of football shirts were given to them … by Nottingham Forest.

24 The name of a sponsor. They think one would spoil the look of their famous blue and red striped shirts.

25 None of them say their shirts are orange. Wolves say they're "gold"; Blackpool and Dundee United say they're "tangerine"; Barnet, Motherwell and Hull say they're "amber".

26 Red spots! They didn't think it made their players look like they'd caught the measles, they thought they made them look bigger and beefier.

27 They had a white sash, which started at one shoulder and crossed to the opposite waist.

Nutty nicknames

Team names – like Liverpool, or AC Milan – usually tell you exactly where in the world the club play. But sometimes they tell you more about the team's origins or famous fans. For instance…

28 What have Crewe Alexandra – a team who've never been in the top division in England – got in common with Spanish giants Real Madrid?

Answer:

28 They both have royal connections. Crewe were just Crewe until they added the second part of their name in honour of Princess Alexandra (and, at the same time, became the only British team with the letter "x" in their name); and Real Madrid were just Madrid FC until fan King Alfonso XIII decreed that they should have Real (which means "royal" in Spanish) tacked on to the front.

A team's nickname can tell you a lot, too. Scottish league club Partick Thistle gained one from comedian Billy Connolly. He said that when he was a boy, the team were so spectacularly unsuccessful at scoring goals that after weeks of listening to the football results he thought their real name was Partick Thistle Nil!

Separate the facts from the fiction in this quiz about club nicknames. Are these explanations true? Or nutty nickname tales?

29 Everton's nickname is "The Toffees" because their players believed that sucking toffees before a match and at half-time gave them extra energy. **True or false?**

30 Brazilian club Fluminense were nicknamed "Face-powder" because their players used to wear make-up. **True or false?**

31 Sheffield United were nicknamed "The Blades" because their early teams used to cut through the opposition. **True or false?**

32 Arsenal became known as "The Gunners" because the word "Arsenal" means a place where guns are made or stored. **True or false?**

33 Charlton Athletic's nickname "The Addicks" came from the owner of a fish and chip shop. **True or false?**

34 The name of the Chilean club Colo Colo is itself a nickname. It means "wild dog". **True or false?**

Answers:
29 False. The club was formed in 1878 (as St Domingo's FC) at a meeting held in a pub. The nickname arose from the fact that next door to the pub was a sweet shop called "Ye Ancient Everton Toffee House".

30 True. The club was formed by a number of wealthy, upper-class Britons. This was in 1902, a time when wearing white face powder was very fashionable for gentlemen! Nowadays Fluminense's players don't wear the stuff – but the fans do! It's to show who they're supporting.

YOU ONLY NEED THE POWDER, Y'KNOW

31 False. Sheffield was world-famous for its steelworks which turned out cutlery sets by the million – spoons, forks … and very, very sharp knives!

32 True. The club's first players all worked at the Woolwich Arsenal in London, turning out guns and explosives. (Did that make them hot-shots?)

33 True. Charlton's players were the owner's best customers.

34 Half false … and half true. Colo Colo is the Chilean nickname for a wild *cat* – and was chosen as the team's name because the five players who formed it in 1925 were just that: really wild! They'd been in a big argument at their previous club and had walked out to start their own.

Gruesome grounds

Nowadays even the lowliest football clubs are playing at swish new grounds. It wasn't always this way. Most of them played their first games on commons or in fields before finding a ground of their own.

Some took ages to find a ground. Bolton Wanderers started out in 1874 calling themselves just "The Wanderers" for the simple reason that for six years they'd been continually wandering around trying to find a pitch to play on regularly. Eventually they settled, though – at a ground named Burnden Park. What did Burnden Park used to be? Find out over the page.

Match these teams' grounds to what used to be there before. The names may give you a clue – and they may not!

Answers:

35 c) The Romanies had to be forced off the land, though – so one of them put a curse on the club, saying they'd never win the FA Cup!

36 h) The site itself was just waste ground, but a new pitch was laid on top of ash from local coalfields. This helped produce grass so lush that in the 1970s the owners of Wembley Stadium, who'd allowed a horse show to ruin their grass, asked Doncaster if they could buy their pitch and transport it to London!

37 a) So when the crowd shouted "rubbish", they didn't always mean the team!

38 g) Southampton really splashed out on their new ground!

39 f) Which may explain why the Germans have so often been high flyers!

40 d) That's why it's called "Park of the Princes"!

41 b) The word "pittodrie" is Gaelic for dung heap.

42 e) In 1914 the pitch was dug up – and a load of graves discovered. None of them belonged to referees, though. They all dated back to Anglo-Saxon times.

Ground improvements

This is a typical football ground today. Imagine it's the year 1890, though. Which of these features would have been around then?

Answers:

43 Yes. The crossbar had been introduced in 1875.

44 No. Penalty kicks weren't invented until 1891.

45 No. Goal nets weren't used until 1891 either.

46 Yes. The first floodlit match was played at Bramall Lane, Sheffield on 14 October 1878. A crowd of 12,000 turned up to watch, over twice as many as attended the FA Cup Final that year!

47 Yes. Corner flags were invented in 1872.

48 No. Aberdeen were the first British club to build a dug-out, in the 1920s. Their manager, Donald Coleman, wanted to get closer to ground-level so he could study his players' footwork!

49 No. Scottish club Celtic first installed a press box in 1894.

Strange stadiums

Very strange things have happened at some stadiums – and we're not just talking matches which finish 19-18 and see eight players sent off for kissing. Use your skill and judgement to make the right choice from these eerie events...

50 Fans who watch Arsenal's matches from the North Bank at Highbury are sitting on top of the last resting place of what?

a) A HORSE AND CART

b) A RED LONDON BUS

c) WHO, ME? AN ARSENAL SUPPORTER

51 One of the goalmouths at Celtic's ground, Parkhead, is supposed to be haunted. Who is the goal-hanging ghost?

a) A Rangers striker who missed a crucial penalty.

b) A past Celtic goalkeeper.

c) A referee who was brained by a bottle.

52 Blackpool's ground at Bloomfield Road is reputed to have had regular visits from whom?

a) Queen Victoria.

WE ARE NOT AMUSED. WE ARE LOSING 5-0

b) Adolf Hitler.

c) Admiral Lord Nelson.

53 In their early days at The Dell, Southampton added a special section to their grandstand. What was it for?

a) The police to hide in.

b) To seat any sailors who happened to be in Southampton port on a match day.

c) To keep their fans' bicycles dry.

54 In 1963 Halifax Town threw open the gates to their ground and let people in to do what?

a) Ice skate.

b) Swim.

c) Buy any bits they wanted.

IT'S MY SLIDE TACKLE!

Answers:

50 a) When the North Bank was being built the public were invited to bring rubbish along to help fill in a hole. One helpful man is said to have backed his horse and cart too close to the hole – and they both fell in. The poor horse was killed, so the owner decided to have it buried there. (Let's just hope it wasn't a Tottenham Hotspur fan!)

51 b) His name was John Thompson. Playing for Celtic against Rangers in 1931 he fractured his skull diving at a player's feet and died in hospital the same day. He was 23 years old.

52 c) Nelson is supposed to have haunted the ground because wood from his flagship *Foudroyant*, which had sunk near Blackpool pier, had been recycled to help build parts of the ground. (Perhaps the Admiral wanted it back and they wood-n't let him have it?)

THEY NEED TO GET THE BALL DOWN THE WING

YOU SAID IT!

53 c) Southampton believed in looking after their supporters wheely well!

54 a) The winter of 1963 was awful. With the ground frozen and covered with ice, skating was all it was suitable for!

Battle grounds

Football grounds aren't always theatres of dreams. In 1916 Hartlepool United claimed a frightful first: the first football ground to be bombed. The First World War was on and German airships flying over Britain had dropped their load all over the ground.

During the Second World War some grounds were used for waging war and some had war waged on them. Match the left- and right-hand sides of these sentences to find out what happened where.

55, Coventry's ground at Highfield Road...

56, The Olympiastadion in Berlin, Germany...

57, The car park of Tranmere Rover's ground, Preston Park...

58, The Ernst-Happel stadium in Vienna, Austria...

59, The stand at Exeter City's ground...

ⓐ ...was bombed so badly it had to be rebuilt and wasn't fit to be used until the 1960s.

ⓑ ...was used to hold people before they were sent to prison camps.

ⓒ ...was used as living quarters by soldiers. They practised their marching on the pitch!

ⓓ ...was bombed, but although three bombs landed on the pitch, the stands escaped almost undamaged.

ⓔ ...was used to send up black smoke to confuse bombers.

Answers:

55 d)

56 a) It's now where the German Cup Final is played every year.

57 e)

58 b) It was also bombed and had to be rebuilt. Rapid Vienna and FK Austria have both used it as a home ground.

59 c)

Fanatical fans

Some fans are more fanatical than others. Labour politician and twice Prime Minister Harold Wilson, a great Huddersfield Town fan, often said he knew more about football than politics (and every non-Labour voter agreed with him!). More recently, pop singer Liam Gallagher wouldn't let Manchester United star Ryan Giggs have free tickets for one of his group's concerts – because Gallagher was a Manchester City fan.

Have you the passion of a fanatical fan? Find out with this quiz.

60 You're a Newcastle fan and, in 1988, Paul Gascoigne is your star player. What do you throw at him when he comes on to the pitch?
a) Liquorice allsorts.
b) Jelly babies.
c) Chocolate bars.

61 You're a West Ham fan and Paul Ince used to be one of your team's top men before he left to join Manchester United. What do you do whenever he comes back to play against West Ham?
a) Boo loudly.
b) Cheer loudly.
c) Ignore him completely.
62 You're David Beckham's dad. What do you do when he scores his first goal for Manchester United?
a) Cry tears of joy.
b) Head-butt somebody.
c) Faint.

63 You're a Denmark fan who is horror-struck because your star player, Brian Laudrup, has decided to retire from international football. What do you do?

a) Organize a petition begging him to stay.

b) Sell your Brian Laudrup photo collection.

c) Camp outside his house until he changes his mind.

64 It's 1961 and your team, Preston North End, have just been relegated. What do you do?

65 It's the 1980s and you're a Crystal Palace fan singing your favourite song about the team's captain, Jim Cannon: "*When Jim goes up to lift the FA Cup, we'll be _____ , we'll be _____ !*" What's the missing word?

a) Glad.

b) There.

c) Dead.

66 You're an Italy fan in 1966 and your team has just arrived home from England after playing in the World Cup finals. What do you throw at them?

a) Flowers.

b) Tomatoes.

c) Money.

67 You're an Aberdeen fan in 1980 and you've just been stopped for trying to smuggle something into the ground. What is it?

a) A bottle of beer.

b) A thermos flask.

c) A barrel of rum.

68 It's 1996 and Rangers have become Scottish League Champions. What do you steal from their ground as a souvenir?

THE PENALTY SPOT

A FLAG

A GOAL, COMPLETE WITH NET

69 You're a fan of Brazilian team, Flamengo. They've lost eight games on the trot. In their previous match only you and 730 other faithful fans turned up to watch them play in the huge Maracana Stadium. How many are there with you for the next game?

a) 51,999.

b) 519.

c) 51.

70 You're a fanatical Derby fan. It's May, 1983 and your team is playing Fulham in the final match of the season. Both teams need to win to gain promotion. With just 78 seconds left Derby are winning 1-0 when the referee blows his whistle for an offside. Thinking it's full time, you – and all the other Derby fans – invade the pitch causing the referee to abandon the match. What happens afterwards?

a) The game is replayed and Fulham win.

b) The game is replayed and Derby win.

c) Derby are declared the winners of the abandoned game.

Answers:

60 c) Gascoigne had appeared on TV saying he loved Mars bars, so the fans made sure he had plenty to help him work, rest and play.

61 a) Not simply because he left West Ham – but because he was photographed in a Manchester United shirt before he'd even been transferred!

62 b) It was an accident. In his excitement, Mr Beckham butted the fan behind him.

63 a) then **c)** A fan organized the petition, then travelled from Denmark to London where Laudrup was playing for Chelsea. It didn't make any difference.

64 a) A coffin was carried through the town, followed by 30,000 fans – a bigger crowd than Preston got to watch them play!

65 c) And they could well be right. Crystal Palace were losing finalists in 1990, but they haven't won the FA Cup yet.

66 b) The team had been humiliatingly beaten by North Korea and the tomatoes made sure the players had red faces about it!

67 b) A ban on fans bringing drinks into matches (because too many had been getting drunk and causing trouble) really annoyed some Aberdeen fans. Their ground is the most northerly league ground in Britain and they didn't want to bring in beer – they wanted to bring in their flasks of soup to keep warm!

68 b) It wasn't just any old flag, it was the Scottish League Championship flag – but whether it was stolen by a Rangers fan or a Celtic fan isn't known!

69 a) Flamengo's president, Kleber Leite, promised the fans that if the team didn't win they'd get their money back! So 51,999 turned up – and saw a free match as Flamengo lost 3-2!

70 c) The game wasn't replayed because it was decided that Fulham wouldn't have equalized in the time left. (Of course they wouldn't – not with all those Derby fans blocking the goal!)

FOUL FOOTBALLERS

Terrible training

To be a top footballer you have to be determined to look after your body at all times by eating the right foods and not staying out late. That's the theory, anyway, but players *are* only human...

Answer these questions about footballers' human weaknesses.

71 Steve Nicol was said by his Liverpool team-mate Mark Lawrenson to be a walking advertisement for the benefits of what sort of food? (Hint: rubbish!)

72 When the Watford player Luther Blissett moved to Italian club AC Milan what food did he say he missed most? (Hint: snap, crackle and pop)

73 The Brazilian international, Socrates, worked his way through three of these every day. What were they? (Hint: surprisingly, he didn't get puffed out)

Answers:

71 Junk food.

72 Rice Crispies. This may be why Blissett didn't have much snap, crackle or pop himself. AC Milan sold him after a year.

73 Packets of cigarettes. He obviously didn't ask himself if he was being sensible. If he had, he'd have definitely told himself to give up – because Socrates was a qualified doctor!

Injury time

Players know that running, jumping, kicking, heading and diving can all cause injuries – especially when they do them to each other!

74 Arsenal FC recognized football was a dangerous game. The club hadn't been going long and money was in short supply but still they invested in some equipment for getting an injured player off the field quickly so that he could receive treatment. What sort of equipment?

a) A stretcher.

b) An ambulance.

c) A milk cart.

Answer: 74 c)

75 Some players even have problems before the game kicks off – Manchester United's Ole Gunnar Solksjaer, for instance. What health problem does he know he'll have to contend with in every game?

a) He's colour blind.

b) He's got one foot bigger than the other.

c) He's allergic to grass.

Answer:
75 c) Yes, you could say grass gets right up his nose!

Let's hope you're not injury-prone, because these questions are all about nasty things that have happened to footballer's frames. The answer to all but one of the questions is a part of the body!

76 In 1963, Rodney Marsh of Queens Park Rangers headed a goal in a match against Leicester City. What did he damage?

77 In April 1980, ex-Arsenal striker Charlie George tried tackling a lawnmower in his garden at home. What did he lose?

78 What did ex-Fulham and Spurs player Alan Mullery damage while he was brushing his teeth?

79 In 1971, Leeds United were on the point of buying West Bromwich Albion player Asa Hartford when his medical examination revealed that he had a possible hole in his what?

WE MAY HAVE A PROBLEM

80 What did Arsenal striker Alan Smith lose during a 1984 match against Stoke City, only for them to be found and returned to their rightful position after the game?

81 What did Manchester United goalkeeper Alex Stepney break during an impressive performance on the pitch?

82 It's not always essential for a footballer to have every part in full working order. What was Chelsea forward Bob Thomson missing when he played in the 1915 FA Cup Final?

83 Ryan Giggs bought a new bed because he thought his old one might be giving him a pain in the – what?

I THINK I KNOW WHAT YOUR PROBLEM IS, SON...

84 What did England forward Trevor Francis swallow while he was playing for Italian club Sampdoria in 1985?

85 And finally, what part of Gordon Durie's body was injured when he collapsed while playing for Tottenham in October 1992?

Answers:
76 His eardrum. He didn't only head a goal, he headed a goalpost as well. It left him permanently deaf in one ear.
77 A finger.

78 He strained his back – which must have made him fed up to the back teeth!

79 His heart. Leeds pulled out of the deal so Hartford signed for Manchester City instead – and played without a problem.

80 Three teeth. They were knocked out when he was fouled, found after a search through the grass, then fixed back in his mouth in hospital.

81 His jaw. He did it shouting at his defence!

82 An eye. (Which may have meant he shed fewer tears afterwards – Chelsea lost!)

83 Leg. Giggs had persistent hamstring problems and thought changing his bed might be the answer.

84 His tongue. It happened after a clash of heads and could have been very serious. Francis stopped breathing and had to be revived with the kiss of life.

85 None at all. Durie became the first player to be found guilty of pretending to be injured in an attempt to get an opponent sent off.

There's one part of a footballer's body that is best kept under cover, though – because if it isn't, they're likely to get in trouble. Like…

● Arsenal defender Sammy Nelson, who showed his to the crowd during a match with Coventry City in 1979 and was banned for two games.

● Robbie Fowler of Liverpool, who revealed his in 1995 to Leicester City's fans and was fined £1,000.

● Nine Wimbledon players, who were each fined £750 (and the club £5,000) for displaying theirs at a testimonial match for Leeds United striker Alan Clarke.

85a What was the offending part of the body in each case?

Answer:
85a Doctors call it the gluteus maximus. Everybody else calls it the bum.

Oy! Wossname!

A lot of the players must have to keep telling themselves: "Kicks and thumps may give me lumps, but names will never hurt me." Because putting up with being called names by spectators is as much a part of being a professional footballer as dodging foul tackles.

Can you replace the WOSSNAMEs to complete the nicknames for these well-known players?

86 Mop-haired Manchester United winger George Best, after helping his team whack Portuguese side Benfica in 1966: "El WOSSNAME".
87 Wild-galloping Liverpool defender Emlyn Hughes: "WOSSNAME Horse".

88 Chelsea and Manchester United midfielder, and lover of the sideways pass, Ray Wilkins: "The WOSSNAME".
89 Ace but "mad as a brush" player Paul Gascoigne: "George Best without the WOSSNAME".

90 Small but impressive Liverpool striker Michael Owen: "WOSSNAME Gem".

91 Talkative and chirpy West Ham forward Johnny Byrne: "WOSSNAME Byrne".

92 Long-haired Italian star forward Roberto di Baggio: "The Divine WOSSNAME".

93 Tough but small Leeds midfielder Bobby Collins: "The Pocket WOSSNAME".

94 French winger David Ginola, in the days when he was a tricky but gangly youngster: "WOSSNAME-WOSSNAME legs".

95 Not exactly slimline Liverpool goalkeeper Tommy Lawrence: "The flying WOSSNAME".

96 England midfielder – famed for marking opponents out of the game – Nobby Stiles: "The WOSSNAME".

In case you need them, here are the words to fill in the gaps (in the wrong order, of course!): Assassin, Battleship, Beatle, Brains, Budgie, Crab, Crazy, French-stick, Midget, Pig, Ponytail.

Answers:

86 Beatle.

87 Crazy. In his first game for Liverpool his manager told him to do something crazy to get the crowd on his side – so he rugby-tackled an opponent.

88 Crab.

89 Brains.

90 Midget.

91 Budgie.
92 Ponytail.
93 Battleship.
94 French-stick (if you speak French it was actually "jambes des baguettes").
95 Pig.
96 Assassin. Stiles got the nickname after he'd helped England beat Argentina in a violent 1966 World Cup quarter-final – from the Argentine newspapers!

Tricky transfers and mad money

Players are a bit like diamonds; clubs hope they're going to shine … and that they're going to be worth a lot when they decide to sell them!

But players aren't always transferred from one club to another for money. There have been times when a hard-up club has offered or received something entirely different by way of a transfer fee…

Sort out the true transfer fee in these silly swaps:

97 When striker Tony Cascarino moved from Crockenhill to Gillingham in 1982 the transfer "fee" was a set of…

98 When Hughie McLenahan joined big spenders Manchester United in 1930 they "paid" Stockport County a "fee" of three...

a) Pitch rollers.

b) Season tickets.

c) Freezers of ice cream.

99 When a player named Jock Spelton joined Holt United from Moss End, the transfer "fee" was 30 sheets of...

a) Corrugated iron.

b) plywood.

c) Cotton – for a bed.

100 When William Wright joined Blackpool in 1951 the transfer "fee" was a set of...

101 When, in 1937, an Aston Villa player joined Gillingham, the transfer "fee" was...

a) A typewriter.

b) Three used turnstiles.

c) Three jars of weed killer.

102 When Daniel Allende joined Uruguyan club Central Espanol the transfer "fee" was...

a) 550 beef steaks.

b) 1,000 pizzas.

c) 365 omelettes.

Answers:

97 a)

98 c) Mind you, Stockport turned it into money by selling it at a fund-raising bazaar.

99 a)

100 b)

101 a), b) and **c)** ... plus two goalkeeper's tops and an assistant trainer! Was the player worth the fee? Can't say. Nobody remembers who he was!

102 a) It was paid at the rate of 25 steaks per week!

One of the oddest transfers didn't involve players at all. When the tiny Croatian fourth-division team Dugo Selo pulled off a giant-killing act by beating FC Croatia Zagreb in the National Cup, the Dugo Selo president was faced with a problem – how to pay his players the bonus (of about £38 each) they'd been promised if they won.

103 What did he "transfer" to raise the money?

a) Two trophies.

b) Two pigs.

c) Two footballs.

Answer:
103 b) Presumably the club didn't have enough money in their own piggy bank!

I've gotta get out of this place!

Sometimes it's not a matter of money. A player may feel he can't stand it at a club a minute longer, let alone run around and play for them. On the other hand, he may not fancy a move to another club because *they're* not fancy enough.

It can happen the other way round as well, of course. A player may still be happy to put on his boots for the club but all they (or his team-mates) want is to see him booted out!

Match the two halves of these statements to reveal some truly tempestuous transfer tales...

104: STAN BOWLES WANTED TO LEAVE QUEENS PARK RANGERS IN 1975 BECAUSE HIS WIFE...

105: IN 1980, KEVIN KEEGAN DECIDED NOT TO JOIN ITALIAN TEAM JUVENTUS BECAUSE HIS WIFE...

106: WELSH STRIKER IAN RUSH WAS DELIGHTED TO LEAVE JUVENTUS IN 1987 BECAUSE HE...

107: PLAYERS AT DUTCH CLUB PSV EINDHOVEN WERE HAPPY WHEN THEIR BRAZILIAN TEAM-MATE ROMARIO LEFT BECAUSE HE ALWAYS...

108: IN 1988 NOTTINGHAM FOREST MANAGER BRIAN CLOUGH TOLD THE WORLD THAT HIS NEW SIGNING FROM TOTTENHAM, STEVE HODGE, SIMPLY HAD TO BE DELIGHTED BECAUSE HE...

(a) SAID "IT WAS LIKE PLAYING IN A FOREIGN COUNTRY."

(b) ...WAS CALLED A DONKEY BY THE OTHER PLAYERS.

(c) ...WAS WORRIED THAT HE MIGHT BE KIDNAPPED BY LOCAL CROOKS.

(d) ...SAID HOUSES WERE TOO EXPENSIVE IN LONDON.

(e) ...RIOTED IN THE STREETS FOR THREE DAYS.

109: ARSENAL STAR DENNIS BERGKAMP WAS DELIGHTED TO MOVE FROM INTER MILAN BECAUSE HE...

110: FIORENTINA FANS WERE SO DISGUSTED WHEN ROBERTO BAGGIO WAS SOLD TO JUVENTUS IN 1990 THAT THEY...

111: IN 1971, SHEFFIELD WEDNESDAY PLAYER WILF SMITH REFUSED TO MOVE TO CHELSEA BECAUSE HE...

f) ...HAD BEEN "RESCUED FROM HELL".

g) ...COMPLAINED ABOUT THE WEATHER.

h) ...WAS HOMESICK FOR THE NORTH OF ENGLAND.

Answers:

104 h)

105 c) Keegan moved to Southampton instead – where he got attacked late at night while sleeping in his car!

106 a)

107 g)

108 f)

109 b) They changed the name of their worst-player award from "Donkey Of The Week" to "Bergkamp Of The Week"!

HE'S GOT A GOOD KICK ON HIM, TOO!

110 e) They only stopped when the police intervened. (So why did it take the police so long? Were they Fiorentina fans too?)

111 d)

After the game is over

Footballers don't spend *all* their time dressed in colourful outfits. So here's a quiz about the sort of amazing things some players get up to when they're off the field...

Can you identify the missing words in the following statements?

112 In 1996, smartly-groomed French star David Ginola won the title "_____ of the year".

113 It is said that once, after a game, Sheffield United's huge goalkeeper in the 1900s, Bill Foulke, once arrived back at the team hotel first ... and ate his dinner, as well as _____ .

114 Arsenal striker Denis Bergkamp won't travel anywhere by ____ .

115 Arthur Wharton, who played for Preston North End in the 1880s, held the world record for the _____ .

116 Most Romanian players carry a _____ .

117 A Japanese player gave up the game and became a _____ – all because he'd scored an own goal.

118 Blackpool's 1953 Cup Final hero, three-goal Stan Mortensen, was made a Freeman of the town in 1989 for selling his _____ to help raise money for the club.

119 Italian star Fabio Galante injured two youngsters by throwing a _____ from his hotel room window.

Need help before you blow for full-time? Here's the list of missing words: *aeroplane, six others, water-bomb, gun, hairstyle, medals, monk, 100-yard sprint.*

Answers:

112 Hairstyle. If Ginola had scored a goal for every time his shoulder-length locks appeared on TV in a shampoo advert he'd have won a lot more football awards.

113 Six others. Foulke's nickname wasn't "Fatty" for nothing!

114 Aeroplane. After a scare during a flight in 1994, Bergkamp refused to fly again. If he can't get to a game by car or train (or on foot!) he doesn't play.

I SEE DENNIS RAN TO THIS ONE

115 100-yard sprint. Wharton was a champion sprinter and an all-round amazing character. He also played cricket and rugby and was the first black professional footballer.

116 Gun. In 1998, after a number of attacks, players began carrying them for self-defence. In one incident, Stelian Carabas of National Bucharest was only rescued from a would-be assailant by team-mate Gheorge Butoiu waving his gun under the man's nose!

117 Monk. Feeling disgraced at letting his side down, the player went off to live in a monastery – but not until he'd burnt his boots to a cinder!

118 Medals. So devoted was Mortensen to Blackpool that when they were struggling for money he auctioned his precious medals to help out.

119 Water-bomb. Galante said he'd been aiming the bomb – a balloon filled with water – at two of his team-mates for a joke but he'd missed and it had gone through the windscreen of a car the youngsters were sitting in. Could a footballer have been such a bad shot? Well, Galante was a defender!

If you weren't a footballer...

Star players are often asked what job they think they would have been doing if they hadn't become a professional footballer – and the answer they often give is that they can't imagine doing anything else. The players mentioned in this next section shouldn't have a problem though...

These players were already working at something else before they turned to football. Fill in the blanks to discover what they were up to.

120 Before becoming an England striker, Ian Wright was a _____ . (Hint: he was a smooth operator)

121 Ex-England winger Chris Waddle's first job was in a _____ factory. (Hint: he didn't beef about it)

122 Pat Jennings, Tottenham's goalkeeper in the 1960s and 70s, worked as a _____ . (Hint: nobody could call big Pat a half-pint)

123 Another goalkeeper, Neville Southall of Everton and Wales, started his working life as a _____ . (Hint: he had trouble keeping clean sheets)

124 At the age of 19 Dan Petrescu, who later played for Chelsea and Romania, was a _____ . (Hint: he always was a good shot)

125 England's Stuart Pearce qualified as an _____ . (Hint: it's not his current job)

126 In 1940, Blackpool's Stan Mortensen joined the Royal Air Force as a _____ . (Hint: he did his best to keep in touch)

These players started out wanting to be footballers but eventually became famous for doing something entirely different. Fill in the gaps with what it was.

127 A young apprentice named Stewart left Brentford to become a _____ . (Hint: he became very pop-ular)

128 A promising Polish goalkeeper named Karol Wojtyla eventually left his home country for Rome and became a _____ . (Hint: he became very pope-ular!)

Every footballer's career has to end some day. Fill in the gaps with what these stars did when their playing days were over.

129 Every Sunday, 1960s Blackpool and England defender Jimmy Armfield became a voluntary _____ . (Hint: it was something he could turn his hand to)

130 Arsenal star of the 1940s and 50s, Jimmy Logie, became a _____ . (Hint: grabbing the headlines was still important to him)

Finding this quiz a bit of a job? Here's the complete list of words you need: *dustman, electrician, milkman, newsagent, organist, plasterer, pop singer, pope, radio operator, sausage, soldier*

Answers:
120 Plasterer.
121 Sausage.
122 Milkman.
123 Dustman.

124 Soldier (in the Romanian army).

125 Electrician.

126 Radio operator. Mortensen was lucky to get back to football at all. One day a bomber plane he was flying in was shot down. All the other crew members were killed.

127 Pop singer. The Stewart in question was Rod Stewart.

128 Pope. Karol Wojtyla is now better known as Pope John-Paul II.

129 Organist – every Sunday, in his local church. On the other days of the week he became a football pundit for the BBC.

130 Newsagent. He had a road-side newspaper stall in London's Piccadilly Circus.

Not guilty, Your Honour!

131 Everton were struggling. Their team were being overrun and it looked like they were heading for defeat. Then, suddenly, the radio commentary increased in volume. Led by their tall striker, Duncan Ferguson, Everton were fighting back. Over came the ball – and Ferguson scored! The commentator went wild:

Why wasn't that a very tactful comment to make?

Answer:

131 Because goalscorer Duncan Ferguson had recently been in jail himself. In 1995, when playing for Rangers, he'd been given a three-month sentence after being found guilty of assaulting a Raith Rovers player during a Scottish League match.

Yes, like people in any walk of life, footballers can get in trouble with the police.

Here are some crooked questions about football folk and crimes they've been accused of committing. You be the judge. Were they innocent or guilty?

132 Jan Molby of Liverpool, in 1988: driving offences. **Innocent or guilty?**

133 Rene Higuita, Columbian goalkeeper, in 1993: helping with a kidnapping. **Innocent or guilty?**

134 Bobby Moore, England's captain, in 1970: stealing a bracelet. **Innocent or guilty?**

135 David Hillier of Arsenal, in 1995: stealing a bag. **Innocent or guilty?**

136 Alfredo Di Stefano of Real Madrid, in 1963: taking part in a kidnapping. **Innocent or guilty?**

137 Jeff Astle of West Bromwich Albion, in 1968: selling FA Cup Final tickets on the black market. **Innocent or guilty?**

138 George Graham, when manager of Arsenal, in 1995: taking money for arranging a transfer. **Innocent or guilty?**

139 Peter Swan, England and Sheffield Wednesday defender, in 1964: fixing a match so that he could win a bet. **Innocent or guilty?**

140 AC Milan, in 1973: bribing a referee. **Innocent or guilty?**

141 Aston Villa, in 1895: stealing the FA Cup. **Innocent or guilty?**

47

Answers:

132 Guilty. He was imprisoned and missed the opening part of that season.

133 Guilty. He was sentenced to four months in prison.

134 Innocent. The incident happened in Bogotá, Colombia, when England were on their way to the World Cup finals in Mexico. A shop assistant was charged with trying to frame him.

135 Guilty. It happened at Gatwick airport, but the magistrate didn't fly off the handle. Hillier was only fined for the offence.

136 Innocent – even though Di Stefano *did* take part in a kidnapping. How? Because he was the victim! Real Madrid were on a tour of Venezuela when some guerrillas grabbed their star forward. He was released, unharmed, three days later.

137 Guilty. Astle's punishment was to lose the captaincy – even though he'd scored the winning goal in the Cup Final.

138 Guilty. Graham's punishment was to be sacked by Arsenal.

139 Guilty. Swan, with two other Sheffield Wednesday players, made sure their team lost 2-0 to Ipswich. They won £100 each, but ended up in jail and the Football Association banned them for life.

140 Guilty. The crooked referee, Christos Michas, was in charge of the European Cup-Winners' Cup Final between AC Milan and Leeds United. The Italian team won 1-0. Leeds? They had three penalty appeals refused and a man sent off!

141 Innocent … although they never did return the FA Cup trophy they'd won that season. It was loaned to a shop to display – and stolen! The club were fined £25, just enough to pay for a new trophy to be made.

Don't quote me on that

Nowadays, with interviews after every game, players need to be as quick with their tongues as with their toes. Trouble is, they're not always as skilful with their tongues. They can say some pretty daft things.

The same goes for others, of course. A lot of daft things have been said about players. For instance, when German striker Jurgen Klinsmann left Tottenham after just one year in 1995, leaving the Tottenham chairman Alan Sugar with his shirt as a souvenir, what sweet words did Sugar spout?

I WOULDN'T EVEN WASH MY CAR WITH THAT SHIRT!

Two years later, he had to eat his words as Tottenham signed a striker to help them out of a relegation crisis – a certain Jurgen Klinsmann!

What words of wisdom did these players pass on when perhaps they should have settled for saying nothing? Fill in the gaps…

142 *"I like to _____ anyone I play against,"* said regularly sent-off Vinnie Jones of Wimbledon.

143 *"People deserve something to go out and _____ at on Saturday afternoons,"* said Queens Park Rangers' most entertaining player, Rodney Marsh.

144 *"When you've seen one _____ , you've seen them all,"* said cultured John Trewick of West Bromwich Albion during his club's visit to China.

145 *"I am the _____est man in football,"* claimed Mick Kennedy of Portsmouth in a newspaper article.

I HATE PENALTIES!

146 *"A penalty is a _____ly way to score,"* said Brazilian ace Pele after scoring one for his 1,000th goal in professional football.

147 *"I'll tie his _____s to a corner flag,"* threatened the ever-friendly Vinnie Jones before facing hairy-headed Dutchman Ruud Gullitt of Chelsea.

And what did other people say about these players?

148 *"His _____s wouldn't last a postman his morning round,"* said 1930s star Dixie Dean about frail-looking fellow England international Joe Mercer.

149 *"He's painful to watch, but _____,"* said Luton manager David Pleat about Liverpool's deadly striker Ian Rush in 1983.

150 *"He's so good, he plays as though he's a _____ ,"* enthused Everton's manager Howard Kendall about his player Kevin Sheedy.

151 *"We were beginning to think he was only _____ ,"* said Kendall again, this time about his miracle-working goalkeeper, Neville Southall.

If you need some help, here are the words you're looking for: *beautiful, Brazilian, coward, dreadlock, hard, human, leg, shout, upset, wall.*

Answers:

142 Upset.

143 Shout.

144 Wall. (Trewick must have had some wall in his garden, then. He was being shown the Great Wall of China at the time.)

145 Hard. (And one of the daftest; the article got him into trouble.)

146 Coward.

157 Dreadlock.

158 Leg. (Actually, Mercer was one of the hardest-running midfield men in football until his career was ended by ... a broken leg.)

159 Beautiful. (Rush had just banged in five goals against Pleat's side!)

150 Brazilian.

151 Human.

FOUL FOOTBALL MATCHES

Competition quandaries

In the early days, football matches were always friendly matches (even when they were foul friendlies). Then league and cup competitions began. Now almost every country in the world has its own football league and cup competitions. On top of those, there are competitions between clubs in different countries. On top of those, there are international competitions between countries themselves. And on top of those … well, there aren't any competitions on top of those yet – but if life's ever discovered anywhere else in the universe then an Inter-planetary Cup won't be far behind.

YOU'LL HAVE TO GET ON THE SPACE SHUTTLE, MR BERGKAMP

NO THANKS, I'LL WALK

152 When were these ten club football competitions first won? Put them into order, oldest first.

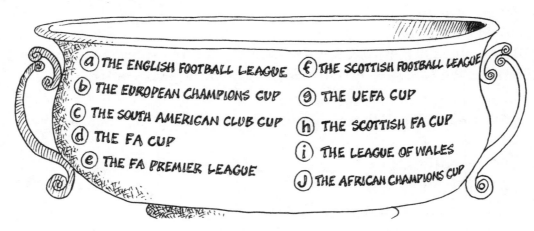

(a) THE ENGLISH FOOTBALL LEAGUE
(b) THE EUROPEAN CHAMPIONS CUP
(c) THE SOUTH AMERICAN CLUB CUP
(d) THE FA CUP
(e) THE FA PREMIER LEAGUE
(f) THE SCOTTISH FOOTBALL LEAGUE
(g) THE UEFA CUP
(h) THE SCOTTISH FA CUP
(i) THE LEAGUE OF WALES
(j) THE AFRICAN CHAMPIONS CUP

Answer:
152 d) (1872), **f)** (1874), **a)** (1889), **f)** (1891), **b)** (1956), **g)** (1958), **c)** (1960), **j)** (1975), **e)** (1993), **i)** (1993)

52

The phenomenal FA Cup

The English FA Cup has seen so many phenomenal games you could write a whole book about it. (Actually, somebody has! Me! It's called *The Phenomenal FA Cup*.) Some parts of the Cup's history are so phenomenal they make you wonder if they're really true...

Which of the following are phenomenal FA Cup facts, and which are foul fibs?

153 A team called The Wanderers once reached the FA Cup Final without playing a match. **True or false?**

154 A player named William Harrison had two reasons to celebrate in 1908. One the same day his team, Wolverhampton Wanderers, won the Cup and his wife gave birth to twins. **True or false?**

155 In the 1946 FA Cup Final a player named Jack Stamp stamped on the ball and it burst. **True or false?**

156 The FA Cup has never been won by a non-league team. **True or false?**

157 A team once played in the FA Cup Final after being beaten in an earlier round. **True or false?**

158 At the end of one Wembley final, the Cup was presented to somebody who hadn't even played in the match. **True or false?**

159 In one FA Cup tie, a Manchester United player spent the last 20 minutes of the game trying not to score. **True or false?**

160 Bert Turner (Charlton, 1946), Tommy Hutchison (Manchester City, 1981) and Gary Mabbutt (Tottenham Hotspur, 1987) all scored for their own team *and* for the opposition in FA Cup Finals and their teams still won the match. **True or false?**

Answers:

153 True. Wanderers were the Cup holders, having won the first-ever competition in 1872. The next season they were allowed to go straight to the Final. The rule was abolished after that.

154 False. Harrison did win with Wolves, but it was his wife who scored a hat trick – she gave birth to triplets, not twins!

155 False. The ball burst as Stamp took a shot. He didn't care. He scored twice and his team, Derby, beat Charlton 4-1.

156 False. When Tottenham Hotspur won in 1901 they were in the Southern League.

157 True. In 1945–46 ties up to (not including) the semi-finals were played over two legs, the only season it's happened. Charlton lost to Fulham in their third round first-leg game but won the tie on aggregate.

THAT'S SOLVED THAT PROBLEM

158 True. At the end of the 2000 Final, Chelsea captain Dennis Wise carried his baby son up with him when he collected the trophy. Not very wise. He might have dropped one of them.

159 True. Manchester United were beating Northampton Town 8-2 and their winger George Best had scored six of them. He said afterwards: "I was so embarrassed I played the last 20 minutes at left back."

160 False. All three players did score for both teams in each Final – but their own teams lost.

The legendary league

The Football League began in 1888–89 with just one division. In 1892–93 a second division was added. A third division came along in 1920–21, and a fourth division in 1921–22.

161 What didn't arrive until 1898–99, six years after the Second Division had been formed?

Answer:
161 Automatic relegation and promotion, in which bottom teams drop down and top teams in the division below go up to take their place.

In other words, the football league has seen its ups and downs! Will you be a promotion candidate or doomed to relegation in this legendary league quiz?

162 In 1996–97 Middlesbrough earned sufficient points to stay in the Premier League but still got relegated. **True or false?**
163 In happier times Middlesbrough, needing just one win to become champions of the old Second Division, were leading 1-0 against Luton Town. What did their manager, Jack Charlton, yell at the players near the end?

164 In 1990, Sunderland lost the old Second Division play-off final and yet they were still promoted. **True or false?**
165 Every season between 1921–22 and 1926–27, Plymouth Argyle came second in their division but weren't promoted once. Why not?

a) Teams wouldn't travel as far as Devon.

b) They lost six play-off matches in a row.

c) Only one team could win promotion.

166 Nowadays the champions of the Football Conference League are promoted to the Football League's Third Division to take the place of the bottom club. But in 1996 the Conference champions Stevenage Borough were told they had to stay where they were because they weren't good enough. **True or false?**

167 On one Saturday, in January 1965, the whole football league programme was cancelled because of what?

a) Bad weather.

b) A funeral.

a) A referee's strike.

...WE SHALL NOT, WE SHALL NOT, WE SHALL NOT BE MOVED...

168 The lowest attendance for a league match was recorded when Leicester City played Stockport County on the last day of the 1920–21 season. Just 130 spectators turned up. **True or false?**

169 The city of Liverpool's two teams, Everton and Liverpool, were both unhappy when Liverpool were relegated from the old First Division in 1954 because they wouldn't be playing against each other. How did they get round the problem?

a) They played a special floodlit friendly match every year.

b) They invented their own competition.

c) They played each other at tiddlywinks instead.

FOUL, REF!

PING!

Answers:

162 True. What pushed them into the relegation zone was having three points deducted for not turning up for a match.

163 a) Middlesbrough were playing away and Charlton really wanted to win the league in front of their home crowd – so he encouraged his players to turn a win into a draw! They disobeyed him, and became champions that day.

164 True. They took the place of Swindon Town who, even though they'd gained enough points to stay up, were relegated from the top division as a punishment for making illegal payments.

165 c) Plymouth were in the (very old) Third Division which was divided into Northern and Southern sections and only the top team in each section won promotion to the Second Division.

166 False. It was the Stevenage *ground* that wasn't good enough.

167 b) The war-time Prime Minister, Sir Winston Churchill, was given a State Funeral so the whole country stopped.

168 False. It was worse than that. The match was played at Old Trafford, miles from either Leicester or Stockport, so only 13 fans watched the match!

169 a) *and* **b)** The two clubs invented their own competition, The Floodlit Challenge Cup which was a sort of serious-friendly match. It was scrapped in 1963. Why? Because that's when Liverpool were promoted and the two clubs started meeting in the league again.

Mad matches

The best football matches of all are those where you just don't know what's going to happen next – like in these mad matches…

The scene is set. The build-up is big. The action is awesome. But the finish is missing. Can you use your skill and judgement to work out what happened next?

170 It's 6th March, 1875. England are due to face Scotland in an international match at the Kennington Oval in London. Kick-off time arrives – but England's goalkeeper Bill Carr doesn't. He's been delayed… *What happened next?* (Clue: "Come on, the ten men!")

171 It's April 1977, and Derby County are playing Manchester City. The referee's whistle shrieks – and, soon after, a groundsman is running on to the pitch with a paintbrush in his hand… *What happened next?* (Clue: he wasn't penalized)

172 It's Wimbledon v Liverpool. Wimbledon win a corner and their man Neil Ardley runs over to take it. He places the ball next to the corner flag, steps back, runs in and… *What happened next?* (Clue: it was certainly a corner kick!)

173 It's 1931, and Chelsea are playing at Blackpool in pouring rain on a freezing cold afternoon. The 6,000 crowd begin yelling "Southern Softies" as a Chelsea player starts shivering with cold. *What happened next?* (Clue: it could be why Chelsea's nickname is "The Blues")

174 It's New Year's Day in 1966, and Chester are playing a Fourth Division match against Aldershot when one of their full-backs, named Jones, breaks his leg. His partner at full-back – another

Jones, but no relation – offers his sympathy, then gets back to the match. *What happened next?* (Clue: it was a cracking game – for all the wrong reasons)

175 It's the 1995-96 season. Leeds United's Gary McAllister, playing against Chelsea, chases after a ball which is going out of play. Unable to stop, McAllister tumbles over the boards surrounding the pitch and lands right in the lap of a Chelsea fan. *What happened next?* (Clue: up for the cup!)

176 It's 1996 and Bolton Wanderers are leading 1-0 against Reading, thanks to a goal by their striker, John McGinlay. Then Bolton's goalkeeper Keith Branagan is sent off and McGinlay takes his place between the posts. *What happened next?* (Clue: not a lot)

And, finally, a what happened before *question.*

177 It's 1986, and Fulham are preparing to meet Liverpool in the second leg of a League Cup tie. Fans who arrive for the match and buy their programme are amused to discover details about what will happen if the two teams are tied on aggregate at the end of the match. Why? *What happened before?* (Clue: double trouble)

Answers:

170 England started the game without a goalkeeper at all! Carr finally arrived – and let in two goals as the teams drew 2-2. Perhaps England should have played the whole game without him: against the ten men Scotland hadn't scored!

171 The groundsman painted a new penalty spot at one end of the pitch. The referee had just awarded a penalty – only to find that the penalty spot had disappeared!

172 Ardley kicked the corner flag and missed the ball altogether.

173 The frozen Chelsea player left the pitch and didn't return. So, one by one, did four more of his Southern softy team-mates! Chelsea ended the game with six players on the field and lost 4-0.
174 Jones number two broke his leg as well.

HERE COMES A COUPLE OF BROKEN "JONES"

175 The Chelsea fan tipped his cup of coffee down the front of McAllister's shirt after giving the Leeds player a piece of his mind.
176 McGinlay didn't let a goal in to complete the remarkable feat of scoring the winner and keeping a clean sheet in the same match.
177 Fulham had lost the first leg game 10-0. Imagining that they could level the scores by beating Liverpool by the same amount was being a little optimistic!

Glorious goals and groanful goals

Goals make a football match. If your team score them, then you're deliriously happy. If the other team score them, then you're as miserable as the Newcastle fan who bought a "David Ginola" replica shirt ... the day before the player left the club to go to Tottenham!

Of course you can still be pretty miserable even when your team do score – at least you can if it's at the wrong end. Own goals have been part of the game from the very beginning: the first official own goal in the football league was scored on the day the competition began in 1888.

Own goals are one of the fouler parts of football for both fan and player. Ask the Aston Villa fans who saw the amazing performance of their defender Chris Nicholl in a match against Leicester City in March, 1976. The final score was 2-2, with Nicholl scoring all four of the goals!

Can you sort out the good goals from the own goals? Each question describes a goal scored in a match. But was it a golden goal hammered into the right end – or a groanful goal thumped into the wrong end?

178 Liverpool v Blackburn, 1995. The ball trickled along the ground towards Blackburn's goalkeeper, Tim Flowers, hit a lump of grass ... and bounced into the net. **Golden or groanful?**

179 Charlton v Middlesbrough, 1960. High in the air, the ball came over from the wing. For some reason the Middlesborough goalkeeper, Peter Taylor, didn't jump ... and into the net it went. **Golden or groanful?**

180 Queens Park Rangers v Barnsley, 1997. From the edge of the penalty area, Trevor Sinclair of QPR kicked the ball over his head to score one of the most amazing goals the crowd had ever seen. **Golden or groanful?**

181 Manchester United v Liverpool, 1977. The ball whizzed into the penalty box. Manchester United's Jimmy Greenhoff tried to get out of the way – unsuccessfully. The ball hit him and spun into the net. **Golden or groanful?**

182 Nottingham Forest v Manchester City, 1990. City's goalkeeper Andy Dibble was gazing around, deciding what to do next, the ball balanced on the palm of his hand. Seconds later it was in the net! **Golden or groanful?**

183 Leicester v Chelsea, 1954. Two Leicester players, Stan Milburn and Jack Froggatt, stretched for the ball. Both made contact at exactly the same instant – and whizzing into the goal it went. **Golden or groanful?**

184 Charlton Athletic v Derby County, 1992. Darren Pitcher of Charlton played a long ball from near the half-way line to his team-mate Scott Minto, prowling on the edge of the penalty area. Without letting the ball bounce, Minto scored with a fine header! **Golden or groanful?**

185 Liverpool v Wimbledon, 1988. In a furious goalmouth scramble, the ball was kicked off the Liverpool line only to be headed straight back into the net. **Golden or groanful?**

186 Fulham v Sheffield Wednesday, 1961. Fulham kicked off. They played the ball coolly from man to man – until Fulham's captain Alan Mullery slid the ball into the net before a Sheffield player had even touched it! **Golden or groanful?**

187 Barrow v Plymouth Argyle, 1963. With the score at 0-0, Ivan Robinson put the ball into the net to give Barrow a 1-0 win ... but he wasn't a Barrow player. **Golden or groanful?**

Answers:
178 Golden. It was a mis-hit shot by Stan Collymore of Liverpool; so bad, in fact, that Collymore turned away in disgust and missed seeing the ball go into the net!
179 Golden. The ball went into the net direct from a corner taken by Johnny Summers of Charlton, to make the score an amazing 6-6. And the reason the Middlesbrough goalkeeper

didn't jump? Unseen by the referee, a Charlton player was standing on his foot!

180 Golden. Sinclair had let fly with a stunning bicycle kick.

181 Golden. Greenhoff had been trying to get out of the way of team-mate Lou Macari's shot – and so ended up accidentally scoring the winning goal in the 1977 FA Cup Final as Manchester United beat Liverpool 2-1.

SURPRISE!

182 Golden. While Dibble was dithering, Gary Crosby of Notts Forest headed it off his hand and popped it in the net. (It wasn't a foul, either. The rules say a goalkeeper has to have both hands on the ball before it's wrong to kick or head it out of them.)

183 Groanful. It was a joint own-goal (although they both probably felt quite half-hearted about admitting it!).

184 Groanful. Pitcher's pass was an accidental slice over his head, and Minto's contribution was an accidental header over his goalkeeper's head.

185 Groanful. The header was from Liverpool's goalkeeper Bruce Grobbelaar who'd been lying on the ground when the clearance hit him on the back of the nut!

I HAVEN'T GOT EYES IN THE BACK OF MY HEAD, Y'KNOW!

186 Groanful. Fulham had been passing the ball backwards. Mullery finished the job off by passing it right back past his goalkeeper.

187 Golden. Because though Ivan Robinson wasn't a Barrow player, he wasn't an own-goal scoring member of Plymouth's team either. He was the referee! George McLean of Barrow had taken a long shot which was going wide until it hit Robinson and was deflected into the goal.

Penalty pearls

The easiest way to score a goal should be from a penalty kick. But if that's the case why do so many teams find them so difficult? Notts County, for instance. In a match against Portsmouth in 1974 this is what they did after being awarded a penalty:

- They missed, but were allowed to take it again because the referee ruled that the Portsmouth goalkeeper had moved illegally.
- They then scored, but had to take it again, because the referee said they'd taken it before the goalie was ready.
- So they took it for a third time, and missed!

No wonder some players feel the need to offer penalty-takers some advice...

What was said on these penalty-taking occasions? Replace BLANK by the correct words!

188 Preston North End player Bill Shankly to his team-mate George Mutch as Mutch stepped up to take a penalty in the last minute of extra-time in the 1938 FA Cup Final:

Close your eyes and BLANK it!

189 Burnley player Jimmy McIlroy to Tottenham captain Danny Blanchflower as Blanchflower prepared to take a penalty in the 1962 Cup Final:

Bet you BLANK it!

190 Italian star, Roberto Baggio, when asked to take a penalty against his old club Fiorentina in 1991:

BLANK!

191 The referee to three Portuegesa players after he'd awarded a penalty against their team in a Brazilian league match against Corinthians:

BLANK!

Answers:

188 "Blast". Mutch did — and scored with a shot in off the crossbar to give Preston a 1-0 win against Huddersfield Town. **189** "Miss". Blanchflower didn't — and Tottenham won the game 3-1.
190 "No". Baggio was immediately substituted!
191 "Off". All three were sent off for arguing with him about his decision.

Oh, Referee!

Poor referee. Players argue with him, managers moan about him, spectators bawl at him and his bosses keep on telling him how to do his job. Sometimes the referee answers back, though...

192 Scottish referee Jim McGilvray resigned after saying that his bosses, the Scottish Football Association, were trying to turn referees into what?

Answer:
192 Robots.

FIRST ONE TO CALL ME A NAME GETS EXTERMINATED

Usually, though, the referee soldiers on and puts up with whatever comes his way. And sometimes it can be pretty foul…

Here's a collection of things referees have had to endure. Use the clue you're given to match the referees with their rotten treatments.

193: ARSENAL PLAYER, IAN WRIGHT, CLAIMED THAT ALL REFEREES WERE...
(CLUE: HE WAS WRONG - LOTS OF REFS ARE BIG AND DON'T HAVE MOUSTACHES!)

194: IN A 1976-77 MATCH BETWEEN WEST BROMWICH ALBION AND BRIGHTON, ALBION'S WILLIE JOHNSTON TRIED TO DO THIS TO THE REF.
(CLUE: HE WAS PAID TO DO IT TO THE BALL.)

195: WHEN MANCHESTER CLUBS CITY AND UNITED MET IN 1974, CITY'S MIKE DOYLE AND UNITED'S LOU MACARI TRIED TO DO THIS TO REFEREE CLIVE THOMAS
(CLUE: I'M TALKING TO YOU TWO.)

196: PLAYING FOR SCOTTISH CLUB RANGERS, PAUL GASCOIGNE WAS GIVEN A YELLOW CARD FOR DOING WHAT TO A REFEREE?
(CLUE: A TASTE OF HIS OWN MEDICINE.)

a) SHOWING HIM A YELLOW CARD.

b) LOCKED HIM IN THE CHANGING ROOM.

c) LITTLE HITLERS.

d) KICK HIM.

197: REFEREE'S ASSISTANTS (FORMERLY KNOWN AS LINESMEN) HAVE PROBLEMS TOO. RAMON MOYA, MANAGER OF SPANISH TEAM HOSPITALET, WAS SENT OFF FOR DOING THIS.
(CLUE: A BIT OF LIP!)

198: AFTER ONE CONTROVERSIAL GAME, MUCH-TRAVELLED MANAGER RON ATKINSON SAID THAT HE NEVER EXPRESSED OPINIONS ABOUT REFEREES, THEN WENT ON TO ADD: "AND I'M NOT BREAKING MY RULE FOR THAT..."
(CLUE: A FOOLISH THING TO SAY.)

199: DOUGLAS PARK, DIRECTOR OF SCOTTISH CLUB HEART OF MIDLOTHIAN, GOT SO ANNOYED WITH THE REFEREE DURING THEIR MATCH AGAINST RANGERS IN 1988 THAT AFTER THE GAME HE DID THIS.
(CLUE: HE BOLTED WHEN HE'D DONE IT!)

e) IDIOT (PRAT, ACTUALLY!)

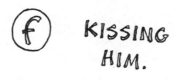
f) KISSING HIM.

g) IGNORE HIM.

Answers:

193 c)

194 d)

195 g) The referee had sent them off and they wouldn't go. So the referee took both teams off until the two players changed their minds.

196 a) The referee had dropped his yellow card, so Gascoigne picked it up and pretended to "book" the referee! Unfortunately for him the referee had also mislaid his sense of humour that day and he showed Gascoigne the yellow card for real.

197 f) In excitement, because his team had just scored an injury-time goal!

198 e)

199 b) He then went off with the key!

Foul fights

Fights and foul play have given referees headaches ever since the game began. For example, how would you have coped if you'd been refereeing this match between deadly local rivals Blackburn Rovers and Burnley way back in 1881?

Decision No. 1:

After a mass punch-up, all the Blackburn players except their goalkeeper walk off the pitch in protest at Burnley's rough play.

200 Do you let the game go on?

Answer:
200 Yes. It's not your fault it's turned into an 11 against 1 match!

Decision No. 2:

Burnley go on the attack, but with not enough Blackburn defenders on the pitch they're immediately caught offside.

201 Do you let the game go on?

Decision No. 3:
But Arthur refuses to take the free-kick because, he says, he's got nobody to pass to!

202 Do you let the game go on?

Here are some foul football fights. Fill in the blanks in the descriptions of what went on.

203 During a 1979 FA Cup tie between Maidstone United and Charlton Athletic, two Charlton players were sent off for _____ each other.

204 Liverpool's Robbie Fowler once messed up team-mate Neil Ruddock's _____ and got thumped because of it.

205 A reporter in Brazil once got hit during a match between Santos and Sport Recife because he tried to _____ two fighting players.

206 When Italian hard-man Claudio Gentile fouled Argentinian Diego Maradona early in a match he growled in his ear, "No, signor, it is not _____ school."

207 A disallowed goal during an international match between Argentina and Peru in 1964 sparked a riot amongst the _____ .

208 During a violent European Fairs Cup match in the 1965–66 season between Leeds United and Valencia, only the intervention of a _____ stopped an enraged Jack Charlton attacking a Valencia player who'd kicked him.

209 An international match between Thailand and Qatar was abandoned by the referee when opposing players started giving each other ____ kicks.

Here are the missing words: *dancing, interview, kung-fu, policeman, punching, shoes, spectators.*

Answers:

203 Punching. Mike Flanagan and Derek Hales forgot they were supposed to be fighting for a Charlton win and started on each other.

204 Shoes. They'd cost Ruddock £200 and he wasn't pleased about having to foot the bill for a new pair.

205 Interview. Yes, the reporter actually stuck his microphone in between two players who were scrapping on the touchline!

206 Dancing. Gentile was no gentle-man!

207 Spectators. It resulted in the worst football crowd disaster ever, with 318 fans being killed.

208 Policeman. Yes, Charlton was held back by the long arm of the law.

209 Kung-fu. (Or should that be Kung-foul?)

Scrambling a win

See if you can scramble a win with this quiz about things that have been said about goals and games and football in general. The quotes have been scrambled so that the <u>underlined</u> part of each quote should be put with another.

210 Much-travelled manager Dave Bassett once said of his shot-shy forwards: *Our strikers couldn't hit a cow's bum with <u>eleven dustbins</u>.*

211 Another manager, Brian Clough, complained about the whack-it-into-the-sky tactics used by many teams: *If God had meant football to be played in the air, he would have put <u>nil</u>.*

212 Famous Brazilian star Pele had a simple description of the game he loved: *Football is <u>glory.</u>*

213 When England star Len Shackleton played his first game for Newcastle United in 1946, he scored six goals in a 13-0 win. Afterwards he said of the poor losing team, Newport County: *And they were lucky to get <u>the beautiful game</u>.*

214 Tottenham had a similar goal-scoring problem in 1976. Complaining about his team's performance, manager Terry Neil said: *We couldn't have beaten <u>a frying pan</u>.*

215 Finally – Danny Blanchflower, the captain of the triumphant Tottenham double-winning team of the 1960–61 season had a different view to everybody else. He said: *Football is not really about winning, or goals, or saves, or supporters – it's about grass in the sky*.

Answers:

210 Bassett actually said: *Our strikers couldn't hit a cow's bum with a frying pan.*

211 Clough said: *If God had meant football to be played in the air, he would have put grass in the sky.*

212 Pele said: *Football is the beautiful game.*

213 Shackleton said: *And they were lucky to get nil.*

214 Neil said: *We couldn't have beaten eleven dustbins.*

215 Blanchflower said: *Football is not really about winning, or goals, or saves, or supporters – it's about glory.*

Decisions, decisions

In charge of every football team is the manager (aka "the Gaffer" or "the Boss"). What does the manager do? Make decisions, that's what the manager does. Who shall I pick for the next game? What tactics shall we adopt? Do we need new players? Who shall I buy and how much shall I pay? Who shall I sell and what are they worth?

Yes, managers are paid to make decisions. Could you be a manager in the making? Find out right now!

Decide what the manager actually did in these situations. (You can choose only one of the options you're given. Be decisive!)

216 It's 1986. Your team are on tour and staying at a posh hotel. One evening, seven of your players are late coming down for dinner. What do you do?

a) Make them go without.

b) Fine them.

c) Make them wash up.

217 You're looking for a new striker. One day a video arrives on your desk, showing very impressive clips of somebody who looks just the man for the job. What do you do?

a) Buy him.

b) Go and watch him play.

c) Accidentally record *Match of the Day* on top of it.

218 You've just been appointed manager of your country and you've got to decide who's going to be captain. What do you do?

219 You decide you want a team of bigger players. What do you do?
a) Buy fitness equipment.
b) Buy a new set of team shorts.
c) Buy bigger players.

220 The night before a big match one of your players disobeys your orders to have an early night and goes out for a drink. Oh, yes – he's also your star player. What do you do?
a) Leave him out.
b) Play the game, then leave him out.
c) Forget it, because your team won the game.

221 Your own son is one of your players. One day another club asks if he's for sale. What do you do?
a) Sell him.
b) Say no.
c) Say no, and give him a pay rise.

222 It's 1994. You've just been appointed manager of your country and everybody wants to know your thinking about the kind of players you want in your team – and those you don't. What do you say?
a) You don't want short players.
b) You don't want players who are colour-blind.
c) You don't want players with long hair.

223 During a match you bring on your substitute and he scores the winning goal. The same thing happens in the next game. What do you do next time?

a) Play him for the full match.

b) Make him substitute again.

c) Sell him while you can.

224 It's close to the end of the match as your ace defender, who's never scored a goal in his career, moves into the attack. What do you do?

a) Cover your eyes.

b) Yell at him to have a shot.

c) Head for the changing rooms.

Answers:

216 b) The team was Manchester United and their manager Ron Atkinson. He was sacked at the end of the year and replaced by one Alex Ferguson.

217 a) Aston Villa manager Brian Little bought Yugoslavian international Savo Milosevic in June 1995 without ever seeing him play live!

218 a) Terry Neil, as manager of Northern Ireland in the early 1970s, not only picked himself but elected himself captain.

219 c) At the start of the 1964–65 season, Liverpool manager Bill Shankly changed his team's strip from red shirts and white shorts to all-red because he thought it made the players look bigger.

220 b) It happened in 1971 to England and West Ham captain Bobby Moore. West Ham lost 4-0 to Blackpool in the FA Cup third round and his club manager Ron Greenwood suspended him after the game.

221 a) Yes, Manchester United manager Sir Alex Ferguson sold his own son Darren to Wolverhampton Wanderers!

222 c) The country was Argentina and their manager was the 1978 World Cup-winning captain Daniel Passarella. His own hair was dark – and short!

223 b) The player was David Fairclough, of Liverpool. During their triumphant years in the late 1970s, manager Bob Paisley used Fairclough so often as a substitute – and Fairclough scored so many goals when he was brought on – that the player was nicknamed "Supersub".

LOOK OUT! THEY'VE SENT ON "SUPERSUB"!

224 c) The manager was Nottingham Forest's Brian Clough, Des Walker was his defender … and as a result Clough missed seeing the only goal Walker scored in a career of 416 games.

Top tactics

One of the manager's top jobs is to work out the team's tactics.

Can he come up with something to surprise the opposition? Like almost falling off the top of the grandstand during a match as David Ashworth, Oldham Athletic's manager from 1906–14, did on one occasion!

Here are some of the things managers have got up to in the past. Every one of them is true, but what you have to work out is: why *did the manager do what he did?*

225 And where else can we start than at Oldham Athletic? Their manager, David Ashworth, really did come close to falling off the top of the flat roof of Oldham's stand during one match. But why was Ashworth up there in the first place?

226 Way back in 1888, Preston North End manager William Sudell regularly had his players poring over a chess set and a snooker table. Why?

227 Thanks to their manager, John Beck, Cambridge United players often had freezing cold water tipped over their heads before a game. Why?

228 Another feature of John Beck's reign at Cambridge United was that he insisted on the grass being left to grow long in the four corners of the pitch. Why?

REMEMBER – WE DON'T TOUCH THE CAMBRIDGE PLAYERS

229 Beck tried the same thing at his next club, Preston North End, but ran into a problem. Why?

230 Birmingham City's manager, Ron Saunders, knew when to put the boot in – he had the soles of his players' boots painted red. Why?

231 In the middle of a European Cup match against Dutch club Ajax in 1960–67 and completely against the rules, Liverpool manager Bill Shankly joined his team on the pitch. Why?

232 In 1981, goalkeeper Neville Southall was banned from training sessions by his manager. Why?

233 During a Blackburn Rovers training session, manager Roy Hodgson showed his defenders how to do a backward roll. Why?

234 Valeri Lobanovsky, manager of the Russian side Dynamo Kiev, picked his teams after looking at his men's performances at playing football computer games. Why?

ZAP! WHOOSH!

HOW IS IT THAT YOUR TEAM IS IN SPACE WITH RAY GUNS?

Answers:

225 It gave him a better view of the game – and because the roof was flat he could run along it and keep up with the play. On the day in question, Ashworth simply got a bit too excited and couldn't stop! Fortunately for him quite a few Oldham supporters were on the roof as well and they managed to grab him in time!

226 Sudell was the first manager to "talk tactics" with his players. To show what he wanted them to do, he used the snooker table as the pitch and the chessmen as players!

227 No, it wasn't because Beck thought his players were a bit grubby – he thought it made them more alert.

228 Beck liked his teams to thump the ball over the opposing defence and towards the corners for his forwards to run on to. Growing the grass long was designed to slow the ball down! It didn't work – with Beck in charge, Cambridge were relegated.

229 There was no grass to grow – at that time, Preston had an artificial pitch! Beck's solution was to make the corners slope upwards by putting heaps of sand underneath them. The tactic still didn't work and with Beck in charge, Preston got relegated as well!

230 Saunders was superstitious and he thought it would bring his team luck. It didn't. With Saunders in charge Birmingham were relegated!

231 To give them some tactical instructions. How did he manage it? No problem – it was so foggy at the time, the referee didn't spot him.

232 Southall was becoming so good, he was making the Bury forwards lose confidence in their shooting ability. In the end they solved the problem in another way – they sold Southall to Everton!

233 It was an accident. Hodgson was demonstrating how he wanted his defenders to back-pedal when the ball was hit over their heads but he tripped over a net full of training balls.

234 Football computer games were part of a "Science of Football" study the Kiev players had to take part in. Lobanovsky obviously thought that a good score meant they could be good scorers!

The sack race

Why are football managers like Santa's helpers? Because they're always being given the sack!

Yes, if you're a football manager you know there's a good chance that one day you'll lose your job. Sometimes it's a surprise – like it was for Sammy Chung, the manager of Doncaster Rovers. He only found out he'd been sacked when he turned up at the ground two hours before his team kicked off for their first match of the 1997–98 season!

Managers who leave clubs haven't always been sacked. Can you spot those who were and those who weren't in this quiz? You're given the facts and all you've got to decide is: sacked or not?

235 It's 1959, and Bill Lambton has been manager of Scunthorpe United for just three days. **Sacked or not?**

236 Bill Nicholson has led his team, Tottenham Hotspur, to a league and FA Cup double, two more FA Cup wins and a European Cup Winners' Cup win. Now his players want more money, and new players want a big (and illegal) payout before they'll sign. Nicholson won't play ball. **Sacked or not?**

237 It's the 1966–67 season and Scott Symon is manager of Rangers. The club are winning nearly all their games. **Sacked or not?**

238 Barry Fry is manager of Barnet. It's four o'clock in the morning and he's just been collared by the police. **Sacked or not?**

239 One of the most successful managers ever was Herbert Chapman of Arsenal. He led Arsenal to two league titles in the 1930s – and his ghost is said to walk the corridors of Arsenal's Highbury stadium to this day. Is that because he was… **Sacked or not?**

240 At the end of a match Brian Clough, manager of Nottingham Forest, angrily clips a few fans round the ear. **Sacked or not?**

241 Another angry manager, Alan Durban of Cardiff City, pours water over a supporter of his team's opponents, York City. **Sacked or not?**

242 Don Revie has just become manager of United Arab Emirates. **Banned or not?**

Answers:
235 Sacked One of Lambton's curious training methods was to get his players doing exercises on a trampoline, the theory being it would keep them supple (and give them extra bounce!).

236 Not. The fed-up Nicholson resigned.

237 Sacked. Not because his team hadn't done well but because, in winning the Scottish League, the SFA Cup, the League Cup, the Glasgow Cup *and* European Cup, their deadly rivals Celtic had done even better!

238 Not. Fry hadn't been moonlighting as a cat-burglar. He'd been unable to sleep so he'd decided to mow the Barnet pitch! That's where the police had found him.

ONE MAN-AGER WENT TO MOW... ♪

239 Not. He'd died while still the manager of Arsenal, catching pneumonia after watching a match.

240 Not. The fans had invaded the pitch at the end of a match.

241 Not. He resigned – but only because he knew he would be sacked. In his two years as manager, Cardiff had been relegated both times.

242 Banned. The problem was that he was also England manager at the time! He fixed up the new job, then resigned. A furious Football Association promptly banned him from managing in England for ten years.

Rhubarb, rhubarb!

You fancy being a football manager one day? Then once you've sorted out tactics and teamwork there's a third T-word you need to practise: talking!

Newspapers, TV interviewers, fans – everybody wants to know what the managers think. And the managers have to say something, even if they really haven't got anything to say.

It must only be a matter of time before a manager gets to his feet and answers yet another stupid question with the words, "At the end of the day ... rhubarb, rhubarb..." So here's a quiz to help you imagine what that will be like!

Here are some of the wise and wonderful things managers have said – except that some of the words have been replaced by the word "rhubarb". Use your skill and judgement to work out what they really said!

243 Liverpool manager, Bill Shankly:

> *Football isn't a matter of life and death. It is much more RHUBARB than that.*

244 Shankly's successor as Liverpool manager, the even more victorious Bob Paisley: *"I've been here during the RHUBARB times too. One year we came second."*

245 To complete the set, Paisley's successor Joe Fagan explained Liverpool's continual success by saying:

> *Our methods are so RHUBARB, sometimes players don't understand them at first.*

246 Nottingham Forest and Derby County manager, Brian Clough: *"In this business you've got to be a RHUBARB or you haven't got a chance."*

247 Norwich manager Martin O'Neill, having second thoughts about predicting promotion for his new club:

> *It was a big statement and I was RHUBARB at the time.*

248 Manchester City's manager Malcolm Allison bragged that his team would:

> *Terrorize RHUBARB with our power and attacking football.*

249 Allison talked/shouted/complained so much he eventually won himself a lifetime ban from sitting on the touchline. Even that didn't shut him up. He complained about the sentence: *"I've served more time than Ronnie Biggs did for the great RHUBARB robbery."*

250 A wiser manager, Joe Mercer of Manchester City (and, for a short time, England), explained why his fellow-managers got so wound up by saying: *"All managers are frustrated RHUBARB."*

251 Much-travelled Tommy Docherty, manager of Manchester United, Chelsea and many others, knew what he was good at, saying in 1967:

> *I talk a lot, on any subject, which is always RHUBARB.*

252 Docherty's tactics as a manager were anything but straightforward, though. Explaining his approach in 1979, he said: *"The only way to survive is by RHUBARB."*

253 There was one group of people Docherty disliked especially:

> *I've always said there's a place for the RHUBARB but they haven't dug it yet.*

254 Republic of Ireland manager Jack Charlton didn't always enjoy interviews. At the end of one he asked: *"Can I go RHUBARB out now?"*

255 Managers aren't happy when they're sacked. John Bond complained on leaving Birmingham City in 1987:

> *You wouldn't treat a RHUBARB the way I've been treated.*

256 Managers get to spend a lot of money, but even that doesn't cheer them up. Manchester City manager Joe Royle once said to West Ham's Harry Redknapp: *"For £1 million all you get is other people's RHUBARB."*

257 It's not only managers who talk rhubarb, club chairmen do it as well – like Ipswich Town's chairman, John Cobbold. After his team had been whacked 10-1 by Fulham at Christmas-time in 1963 he joked:

> *Only our goalkeeper was RHUBARB.*

Stuck for RHUBARB replacements? Here are the words you need: *bad, cheating, dictator, dog, drunk, easy, Europe, football, important, players, press, problems, sober, storming, train*

International football, country versus country, is football at the highest level. World-class football. And so to be the manager of an international squad you've got to be able to talk…

World-class rhubarb

Replace the RHUBARBs in these statements from some England managers…

258 Sir Alf Ramsey, who took his team to the World Cup in 1970 said:

> *We have nothing to learn from the RHUBARB.*

259 Bobby Robson wasn't so sure. In 1988 he said: *"Maybe we're not as RHUBARB as we thought we were."*

260 Things didn't go well for Graham Taylor. After his England team had let slip a one-goal lead to lose 2-1 to Sweden in 1992, he complained: *"We could have done with not having RHUBARB arriving, but you have to have RHUBARB."*

261 Don Revie walked out on England in 1977, saying: *"I sat down with my wife and we agreed that the England job was no longer worth the RHUBARB."*

262 But enthusiasm was Kevin Keegan's strong point, so let's give him the last word:

> *We can end the RHUBARB as it started – as the greatest football nation in the world!*

Still digging around for RHUBARB replacements? Here are the world-class words you need: *aggravation, Brazilians, good, half-time, millennium*

Answers:
258 Brazilians (who promptly won the World Cup!) 259 good
260 half-time 261 aggravation 262 millennium

The Big Day

If you're a player, your big ambition will be to play for your country. However many times you manage it, you always hope you'll have a great game and that it will be a day to remember...

How did these international appearances work out? You decide!

263 GO Smith played centre-forward for England throughout the 1890s and was the first player to win 20 caps for his country. What did he refuse to do during games?
a) Foul an opponent.
b) Head the ball.
c) Help his defence.

264 Blackpool and England goalscorer Stan Mortensen played his first full international match in 1943. What was special about it?
a) He played in goal.
b) He played in a different colour shirt to the rest of the England team.
c) He played in borrowed boots.

COCO WAS THE ONLY PERSON WITH SPARE BOOTS!

265 Bill Nicholson played his first game for England against Portugal in 1951. What happened after just 19 seconds?

a) He scored for England.

b) He scored an own goal.

c) He was sent off.

266 Kevin Hector of Derby County first played for England in 1973. How long did his international career last?

a) 90 games.

b) 90 minutes.

c) 90 seconds.

Answers:

263 b) Smith believed that football was a game that should be played on the ground!

264 b) Because he played for Wales! Mortensen had been picked as a reserve and when Wales turned up short of players (which often happened with games during World War Two) Mortensen played for them instead.

265 a) It was his first touch in international football! Not surprisingly, Nicholson holds the record for the fastest goal scored by a player in his first match. More surprisingly, he also holds the record for the fastest goal scored by a player in his *only* international. Nicholson was never picked for England again!

266 c) Hector was thrown on as a last-gasp substitute with England desperately needing a goal against Poland to win a vital World Cup qualifying match. He scraped the post with a header, England went out of the competition and Hector didn't play for his country again.

Friend or foe?

An international match can be part of a competition, like the European Championships or the World Cup, or it can just be a "friendly" game.

Well, that's what internationals that aren't part of a competition are called…

Sort out the friendly from the unfriendly in this collection of international incidents.

267 It's 1968 and England have just arrived north of the border to play a friendly against Scotland. "Welcome to Scotland," says a journalist to the England manager, Sir Alf Ramsey. Is Ramsey's reply friendly or unfriendly?

268 It's 1936, and England are lining up to play Germany in Berlin. They've been told that when the German national anthem is played they should give the Nazi salute to avoid offending Germany's leader, Adolf Hitler, who is in the crowd. Is the team's response friendly or unfriendly?

269 It's 1952, and France are playing Northern Ireland. Bonifaci, one of the French players, is injured and goes off for treatment. When he comes back to the pitch, what sort of welcome does he receive – friendly or unfriendly?

270 Between 1949 and 1957, how did Colombia treat other international sides? Were they friendly or unfriendly?

Answers:

267 Unfriendly. Ramsey replied, "You must be *@*£-ing joking!"

268 Friendly. Well, friendly in that they did give the Nazi salute. They then went on to give Germany a very unfriendly 6-3 beating!

269 Too friendly! The injured player was allowed back on, even though a substitute had already come on in his place. So France played with 12 men until the mistake was noticed at half-time.

DO YOU GET THE FEELING THEY HAVE MORE PLAYERS THAN US?

270 Unfriendly. Colombia had argued with the international Football Association, FIFA, and so didn't arrange a single international match during those eight years.

Wicked World Cup

It's the biggest, most wicked football competition there is. The World Cup takes place every four years and involves just about every country on the planet.

So here's a wicked quiz with a difference – you're given all the answers! What you have to do is work out which question they're the answer to!

271 The answer is: *A dog named Pickles*. Is the question...
a) Who dug a hole in the middle of a pitch in 1966?
b) Who found the World Cup trophy after it went missing in 1966?
c) Who outran a winger during their opening game in 1966?
272 The answer is: *It bit him*. Is the question...

a) What did a flea do to a World Cup referee in 1978?

THAT LOOKS A BIT FISHY!

b) What did a piranha fish do to a World Cup player in 1978?
c) What did a dog do to a World Cup manager in 1978?

273 The answer is: *He threw it out of a hotel window*. Is the question...

a) What did an England player do with a World Cup medal in 1970?

b) What did an England player do with his dinner in 1970?

c) What did an England player accidentally do with a prize match-ball in 1970?

274 The answer is: *"Ridiculous! Can't we play them again?"* Is the question...

a) What did an England player say after losing a match in 1950?
b) What did an Ireland player say after losing a match in 1950?
c) What did a Scotland player say after losing a match in 1950?

275 The answer is: *They bleached their hair blond.* Is the question…

a) How did Brazilian fans support their yellow-shirted team in the 1998 finals?

b) How did Romanian players celebrate reaching the second round of the 1998 tournament?

c) How did the wives of the 1998 tournament referees show their togetherness?

276 The answer is: *Bare feet.* Is the question…

a) What did Brazil's 1938 forward Leonidas play in?

b) What really annoyed a World Cup referee in 1938?

c) What helped the tournament's top goalscorer in 1938?

Answers:

271 b) The trophy went missing after being displayed at an exhibition and Pickles found it beneath a hedge.

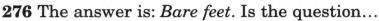

272 c) The manager was Scotland's much-criticized Ally McLeod. When the dog trotted up to him after his team had been knocked out McLeod said, "Ah, my only friend in the world"!

273 a) An upset Alan Ball did this after England had surrendered a 2-0 lead to go down 3-2 to West Germany.

274 a) The player was England's Wilf Mannion. His team had just lost 1-0 to the USA in one of the World Cup's all-time shock results.

275 b) Ten of the eleven players did this. The odd man out was the goalkeeper. He had a reasonable excuse, though. He was bald!

276 a), b) *or* **c)** You couldn't get this one wrong. In 1938 Brazil's Leonidas scored a first-half hat trick against Poland. During the second half the sole of his boot came off and he played for a while bare-footed until the referee objected and made him put his boots back on. Just as well, really. Leonidas finished as the tournament's top scorer and so earned the "golden boot" award. A golden no-boot award would have looked really silly!

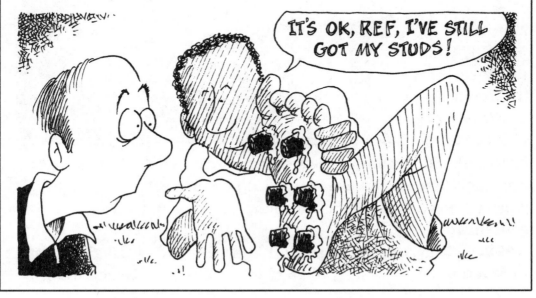

END-TO-END QUIZ

To finish with, here's a quiz to test your all-round knowledge of football. There are questions on clubs, players, goals – everything. They're all different. Except for one thing. They're all fiendishly foul!

277 Bristol Rovers were originally called by a very different name: *Purdown* _____ . Fill in the gap.

| **a)** PIRANHAS | **b)** POACHERS | **c)** PIRATES |

278 TV viewers hoping to watch the highlights of the whole Celtic v Rangers Scottish League Cup Final in 1957–8 only got to see what happened in the first half. This was because the floodlights were too dim. **True or false?**

279 What did Luton Town ban from their home matches in 1986–87?

a) TV cameras.

b) Marching bands.

c) Away team supporters.

280 Barnsley FC were founded in 1888, when they bought their first ground. The man they bought it from laid down a strict condition, saying: "You have to _____ yourselves." Fill in the gap.

a) Behave.

b) Mow it.

c) Wash.

281 In their early days, Grimsby Town's players changed in workmen's huts. **True or false?**

282 When Manchester United arrived in Turkey to play Galatasaray in the 1993–94 European Champions League, they were met by banners saying: *Welcome to _____* . Fill in the gap.

a) Turkey.

b) Defeat.

c) Hell.

283 In 1995, Leyton Orient's ground at Brisbane Road was the first football stadium ever to be used for what?

284 In 1983 the USA launched a campaign for goalkeepers to wear what?

a) Helmets.

b) Shoulder pads.

c) Goggles.

285 In 1901, Liverpool advertised for new players in the sports newspaper *Athletic News*. True or false?

286 In 1970, West Ham's Bobby Moore pulled out of playing in a pre-season friendly because crooks had threatened to kidnap him. **True or false?**

287 In 1881, Sunderland had hardly any money in the bank. They were saved from going bust by one of their supporters selling his prize what?

a) Canary.

b) Red and white roses.

c) Vegetables.

288 Argentinian teams Nacional and Penarol were playing in 1932 when a Nacional shot whizzed outside the Penarol post. What happened next?

a) The ball flattened a spectator, who then started a riot.

b) The ball hit a soldier's rifle, causing it to go off and plug a hole in the Penarol goalie's cap.

c) The ball hit a cameraman's case, bounced back into play and Nacional "scored".

289 London-born England manager Sir Alf Ramsey took lessons to try and get rid of his cockney accent. Is it true or ain't it, mate?

290 Ian Rush was in the Liverpool team that played Arsenal in the 1987 League Cup Final. He scored, but Liverpool lost 2-1. What was unusual about that?

a) Rush was Liverpool's goalkeeper.

b) Until then, Liverpool had always won if Rush scored.

c) Exactly the same thing had happened the year before.

291 In the 1986 World Cup Finals, England's Ray Wilkins was sent off for throwing the ball to the referee. **True or false?**

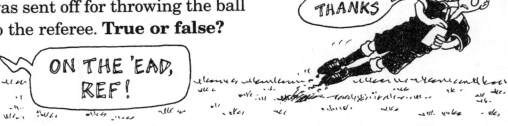

292 What did the 1874, 1878, 1879, 1880 and 1881 FA Cup Finals have in common?

a) One of the teams hadn't had to play a semi-final match.

b) They were all won by the same team.

b) The winning team had lost the year before.

293 Cameroon star Roger Milla started a fashion with his goal celebration. What was it?

294 In an unusual match between Belgian league teams AA Gent and Lokeren in 1994, a penalty was saved by a non-goalkeeper and scored by a goalkeeper. **True or false?**

295 When the FA appointed Don Revie as England manager Alan Hardaker, the boss of the Football League, said, "*You must be _____.*" What are the missing words?

a) *off your heads.*

b) *paying him a fortune.*

c) *really desperate.*

296 After a fight during the 1985 Bulgarian Cup Final, top player Hristo Stoichkov was banned for six months. **True or false?**

297 A goal by Holland's Rob Rensenbrink in 1978 reached a landmark in the history of the World Cup competition. Was it:

a) The 100th goal.

b) The 1,000th goal.

c) The 10,000th goal.

298 In December 2000 the Notts County players had to dodge some unusual creatures on their pitch. What were they?

299 In 1871 it would have been legal to play a match with a football that was as big as a pumpkin or as small as an orange. **True or false?**

300 In 1998 when Thailand met Indonesia in an Asian Tiger Cup game, Thailand won 3-2 with a goal in the last minute. What was unusual about it?

a) It went in off a wild dog that had run on to the pitch.

b) It was scored by the oldest international goalscorer ever.

c) It was a deliberate own-goal.

Answers:

277 b) They only ended as *Bristol Rovers* after another, double, change: to black shirts and the name *Black Arabs*!

278 False. It was the TV cameraman who was too dim. He forgot to take the lens-cap off the camera and the whole second-half recording was lost! (Probably just as well for the Rangers fans: Celtic had won the game 7-1!)

279 c) It was their way of stopping crowd trouble, but all it did was get *them* into trouble. They were thrown out of the League Cup competition because of it.

280 a) Barnsley must have done as he wanted because they've been there ever since!

281 False. The truth is even stranger. They changed in bathing huts wheeled up from a nearby beach!

282 c) It was, too. United were knocked out, had one player sent off and another couple belted by the Turkish police as they headed for the dressing room!

283 b) The ceremony was conducted by a Rev Alex Comfort – who just happened to be an ex-professional footballer.

284 a) Yes, they did know that the goalkeeper is the only player in the team who doesn't head the ball. They wanted to protect them from getting hurt diving at forwards' feet – but didn't think about what nasty injuries the helmets would cause those same feet!

285 True. It was a common thing to do in those days. The same edition also had "players wanted" ads from Sheffield Wednesday, Sheffield United, Preston and Southampton.

286 False. They'd threatened to kidnap his wife.

287 a) It raised £1, and that made all the difference. Besides, in those days £1 for a canary wasn't cheep!

288 c) The "goal" counted because the referee just wasn't snap-py enough to spot what had happened!

289 True, innit!

290 b) And as Rush had played his first game for Liverpool seven years before, and scored an awful lot of goals, that was an awful lot of winning games.

291 False. He was sent off for throwing the ball *at* the referee!

RIGHT! NOW I'M GOING TO THROW THE BOOK AT YOU!

292 a) In 1873, as holders, Wanderers went straight to the final. In the other seasons The Wanderers, Clapham Rovers (twice) and Old Etonians didn't have to play a semi-final because their opponents pulled out for different reasons.

SORRY, WE CAN'T PLAY. IT'S THE GROUNDSMAN'S GRANNIE'S BIRTHDAY PARTY

MANAGER

293 b) Milla had cause to celebrate. At 42 years old, he's the oldest player to have scored in a World Cup finals match.

294 True. Eric Viscaal of AA Gent took over in goal when their keeper was sent off, saved a penalty with his first touch, then scored one at the other end to win the game.

295 a) Obviously, Hardaker didn't think Revie would do well … and he was right.

296 False *and* **true**. He was originally banned for life – but because he was such an important player for Bulgaria it was decided that six months was a long enough ban after all!

I SENTENCE YOU TO A LIFE BAN, SIX MONTHS NOW, AND THE REST AFTER YOU RETIRE

297 b)

298 a) The pitch had been flooded after a tributary of the River Trent burst its banks and the fish came with the water.

When the water went the fish made a bad mistake and stayed behind.

299 True. Until 1872, the match ball could be any size the teams wanted.

Spot the Giant Ball...

300 c) With both of the teams already qualified for the semi-final it was a match neither wanted to win because it meant they'd play favourites Vietnam. So with a minute left, Indonesian defender Mursyid Effendi belted the ball into his own goal! It didn't help. Both of them lost their semi-finals. They were also fined and banned when the tournament was over!

Final score

That's it, full time. If you've been looking at the question numbers as you've gone through the book you'll realize you've been asked 300 questions all together. So, how did you get on?

Over 250	No question about it, you're a top scorer.
125–249	Excellent. More on target than over the bar.
25–124	Not bad. A bit of shooting practice needed.
0–24	Oh dear. What a foul performance!

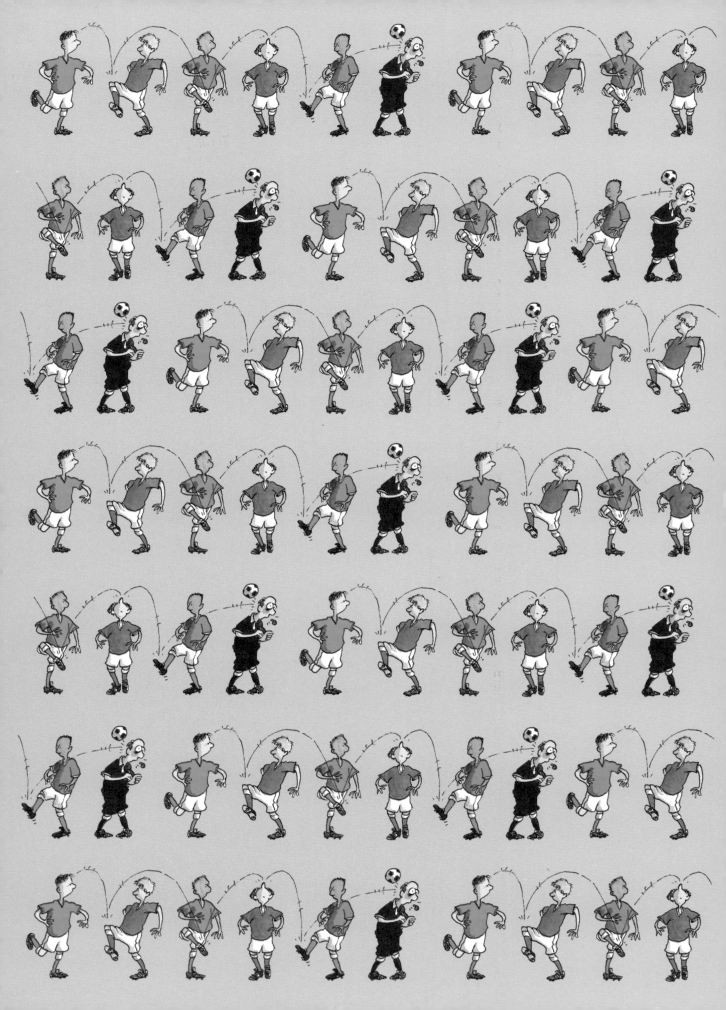